Barbara Wimmer

DJ Culture and Music Journalism

GRIN Publishing

Imprint:

Copyright © 2000 GRIN Verlag, Open Publishing GmbH
Print and binding: Books on Demand GmbH, Norderstedt Germany
ISBN: 978-3-640-12807-5

This book at GRIN:

http://www.grin.com/en/e-book/100611/dj-culture-and-music-journalism

GRIN - Your knowledge has value

Since its foundation in 1998, GRIN has specialized in publishing academic texts by students, college teachers and other academics as e-book and printed book. The website www.grin.com is an ideal platform for presenting term papers, final papers, scientific essays, dissertations and specialist books.

Visit us on the internet:

http://www.grin.com/

http://www.facebook.com/grincom

http://www.twitter.com/grin_com

Seminar zum Praxisfeld Journalismus: Kulturvermittlung und medialer
Kulturdiskurs
iG 8.1.3.
Prof. Bauer Thomas

Wimmer Barbara

DJ Culture and Music Journalism – a theoretical and practical discourse

DJ Culture and Music Journalism – a theoretical and practical discourse

I.) Introduction

My presentation deals with the term and the existence of a "DJ Culture" as a worldwide phenomenon. DJ Culture does not only exist at one place in the whole world - it is a cultural movement which can be mostly be found in urban and suburban surroundings in the so-called "western-orientated" world. If somebody is interested in this cultural development, he or she can spot it in the United States as well as in Europe. Apart from introducing this phenomenon to you, my task is also to present the existence of DJ magazines and general music magazines located in Austria, Germany and Great Britain. Because of the wide range of musical styles, I reduced my reflection to hip hop & breakbeat culture including the new phenomenon drum'n'bass.

For those of you who have not heard the word DJ yet – it is an abbreviation of the word "disk jokey" and formerly was defined as somebody who presents discs.

II.) DJ Culture – Popular Culture or Subculture?

First of all, it has to be noted that "culture" does not start with Mc Donalds and ends up with chips in front of the daily television program. "Culture" cannot be defined clearly, since there are so many subcultures and divisions throughout the social systems. Especially DJ Culture cannot be put in one category: it often stands between popular culture and subculture. To explain this statement more in detail, I'll give you an example: Until 1979 Hip Hop Music, which has had an enormous influence on DJ action, was a local form of culture inside New York's ghetto – the Bronx. This local community had its own cultural activities: DJ-ing, rapping, graffiti spraying and breakdancing. The black community could develop their own culture without the ideology of the bourgeoisie – they did not care about cultural traditions, they simply were free of any obligations towards society and they used this freedom to develop their own culture.

At this time, Hip Hop Culture was Underground, it only took place in the ghettos of New York City. But a couple of years later, the first tapes left the ghetto and the original style was adapted by some musicians. Until this time, hip hop was only available live as party music or as a tape recording. But soon it got adopted by people who were not part of the original cultural development and spread on vinyl. It reached the masses, also white people got access to hip hop music and throughout the last centuries this style got included into popular culture. The movement became successful, hip hop records have been sold worldwide in large numbers.[1]

This development can be found with many different music styles: To give another example, Disco Music originated in gay clubs. The disco sound was part of a gay community, a gay culture, that had no moral suppressions. The parties at clubs were a way of expressing their sexuality openly. Dancing was used as a body language, dancing becomes a form of submission to the overmasting beat. The beat of disco music makes people dance and wakens their desire.[2]

"Desire, according to this analogy, is more than a physical sensation or a psychological drive; it is an external force that can penetrate and establish control over any number of individuals, drawing them into to a community of submission."[3]

1975 the minority "disco" became mainstream. The Saturday Night Fever broke out with the youngsters who fled in the clubs to dance. A couple of years later, disco music changed into house music which can be regarded as a worldwide phenomenon now, which has progressed and has not disappeared yet. Every Saturday night people can still be found at clubs dancing to the happy house sound.

With every new musical style, a new community, a new subculture, comes into existence. This subculture, firstly part of a restricted community, reaches the masses and becomes mainstream and part of popular culture. The latest development was Techno Music and Culture with its "love, peace & happiness"-attitude adopted from the hippie generation. But whereas the generation of 68 can be described as political, it is often heard that the Techno generation just lives for fun and is not potitical at all. The closeness to a consume-orientated society and the commercialisation of the whole phenomenon is also critized by the bourgoisie and some journalists. Nevertheless, the raving society does not care much about these critiques, because it strictly follows it s attitudes: the body is the message. That's why there

---

[1] Vgl. Poschardt, Ulf: DJ Culture – Diskjokeys und Popkultur. Rowohlt. Reinbek bei Hamburg. Oktober 1997. S.411ff
[2] Vgl. Porschardt, Ulf: ebda. S. 117ff

are no lyrics in the strictly computer-generated songs... the raving nation, which is the latest example of the step between subculture and mass culture, expresses it s messages through the dancing body instead of critical texts.

III.)   The role of Europe in DJ Culture

Now I'll make a short excursion to the role of Europe within the development of DJ culture. Most of the popular sounds originated in the United States, but there are a couple of musicians in Europe who influenced the founders of underground hip hop. Afrika Bambaataa, mixmaster and turntablist of the early hip hop movement, was influenced massively by the German electro-avantgarde called Kraftwerk. They were the first people who dreamed of a strictly technological world, they wanted to realize a fusion of man and machine back in 1977. Kraftwerk's music was an expression of nice and modern music at the same time – their high-tech utopia was a way of dealing with the surroundings. Kraftwerk can be regarded as the first German (and European) B-Boys, they were the first Europeans who had any influence on the development of underground music and DJ culture.[4]

During the last century, the role of Europe changed. More music styles and related underground cultures came into existence, some of them originated in Europe. The existence of drum'n'bass is one of the best examples: Originating from hip hop, breakbeat and the jamaican soundsystem, drum'n'bass developed throughout the last century in Great Britain. At the beginning of the 1990s the local DJs had enough of the sound which always sounded the same, they created something new. Firstly called "hardcore", drum'n'bass can be regarded as the rebirth of the Bronx Hip Hop with exactly the same instruments: two turntables and an MC (Master of Ceremony). The DJs of Bristol and London are the godfathers of drum'n'bass – the European counterpart of the Bronx hip hop movement in the 1970s. This music lives of its fast breakbeat, of its bass sounds which are similar to dub music and of its extremely high-pitched drum-parts. London's club culture got mad for those sounds and therefore this style also left the underground and became popular all over the world. In 1999 Drum'n'Bass Parties were part of every urban surrounding of the "western world". The drum'n'bass sound became mainstream as well.[5]

---

[3] Hughes, Walter: Feeling Mighty Real. In: Rock'n'Roll Quarterly. Sommer 1993. S.10
[4] Vgl. Porschardt, Ulf: ebda. S. 229ff
[5] Vgl. Porschardt, Ulf: ebda. S.422ff

"...Most drum & bass DJs and producers that have been involved in the music scene since the mid-80s cite old skool hip hop, funk and rare groove artists as inspirational figures. However, despite the unquestionable importance of this era of music, there's a whole generation of drum & bass fanatics out there that hadn't even left the womb by 1980: and for them, the influence of that style pales in comparison to that of the 90s rave scene and the current leading drum & bass artists."[6]

In the summer of 2000 the first European Drum and Bass Convention will take place in the north of France – in the middle of Europe. Organized by one of the godfathers of drum'n'bass, all crews, DJs and producer from whole Europe are invited to join this convention. France, Belgium, the Netherlands, Austria, Germany, Finnland and some other European countries have already contacted the organization and their crews want to present their DJ skills at this festival.

IV.) DJ Magazines – representing DJ culture for their consumers

DJ magazines exist as long as DJ culture came into existence. For several reasons I do not want to give an historical overview, but have a look at current magazines. I chose some related magazines with the focus on drum'n'bass, hip hop and breakbeat, which are distributed in Great Britain on the one side and in Germany, Austria and Swiss on the other side.

This one (showing it to the audience) is called "Knowledge" and is published every second month, six times a year. It deals with drum'n'bass labels, producers, DJs on the one side and hip hop DJs on the other side. There are interviews with star DJs, reports on them, reviews of the latest drum'n'bass and hip hop releases, DJ charts, dates and more. One important aspect has to be mentioned here: the magazine does not only tell stories about some famous people, it is much more. It represents breakbeat culture. It brings the street culture to an interested audience. Therefore it is a documentation of the present situation of this specific culture. The magazine is not only made for DJs, it is published for everybody within this culture.

So does the German counterpart of "Knowledge", called "Breakbeat". Its undertitle "drum & bass/hip hop/graffiti" is printed in the same style as on the knowledge magazine and somebody can definitely see a correlation between these magazines. Breakbeat also has plenty of reports, interviews, reviews and in addition to that it has technical tips for DJs, equipment

---

[6] Arnell, Richard: Krust, in: knowledge 2/12. November 1999. Vision Publishing. Bristol 1999

for DJs and producers and – most important in our viewpoint – it presents graffitis in the middle. About 5 pages of the whole magazine are dedicated to the art of spraying which is an astonishing part of hip hop and breakbeat culture. The names of the sprayers are written above the graffiti pictures. I'll come back to this topic in a couple of minutes and present the development of graffiti culture to you.

Before this short excursion, I have to mention that the Breakbeat magazine does finance itself strictly through promotion. Whereas the Knowledge magazine can be bought in cigarette and magazine stores and includes advertisment, the Breakbeat is only available at record shops, fashion shops, stores for technical equipment etc. It is strictly available at places where the target group shops. The promotion of the articles mostly is available at those shops and replaces the advertisement. It informs the readers about new products and also gives a phone number, where this article of desire is available for the consumer. This is an enormous difference to straight advertisement, which does not tell somebody where the desired product is available. This promotion only contains products like DJ equipment, hip hop fashion, CD or Vinyl releases or party dates – it is strictly reduced to the readership of the magazine and it is strictly adressing the cultural group itself.

V.)   Excursion: Graffiti culture

At this point I'll make a short excursion into graffiti art, because it is a huge part of the breakbeat culture and belongs to hip hop music and DJ action.

Graffiti art did not arise over night, it took years of development. It became popular when kids in the United States started to "tag" house walls with their street names and numbers in the 1970s. Some of them tagged the whole city and started to tag police cars and trains, because they got bored quickly. At the beginning, the tagging was more a game than something else, but during the years it got a lifestyle for the writers. They made graffiti arts, developed writing styles and new spray techniques. Graffiti became popular within the community, but also other people liked the art of the writers. But as soon as graffiti became mainstream, many youngsters tried to adopt the original writers and the art got criminalized. It was strictly forbidden to write on walls, trains or cars and you have to pay high fees when you get caught and sometimes you can even be sent into prison for writing on walls. The real artists also got affected by these rules and the graffiti art became underground again.[7]

"When a breakdancer comes off a dance he ends up like this, like that. If you look at the (graffiti) letters, they're doing the exact same thing – it's like a pose – I always hear graffiti artists going "He makes those letters dance". That's what it's like – he gives them animation, life. The letters have a kind of life. Graffiti puts kind of a muscular, acrobatic power into the style of the letters, and I think that's a big part of it."[8]

VI.) Intellectual music magazines – adressing a special target group

Apart from many music magazines which are not worth to be mentioned in a scientific piece of writing, there can be found some which lead an intellectual discourse about popular music. They consist of hardly any advertisement, long reports (feature stories are longer than 2 pages!) and intellectual music reviews. Nevertheless, they differ from special DJ magazines, because their reports are less technique-orientated and more philosophical. They are not only specializing on DJ music, although DJs became more important throughout the last couple of years. Rock, pop, electronica, punk, trash, hip hop – every style which is in the mouths of youth culture is part of these intellectual music magazines. One of the best examples is the magazine "Spex" that calls itself "The magazine for popular culture".

The following quotation is taken from an issue of "Spex":

"The world: a village? Popular music is urging the import/export beyond ethnopop: between cultures, in the universe or in future... "[9]

The feature stories in "Spex" are often longer than two pages and very high-brow language is used by the authors who mainly have a higher education. The layout is done very professional, there are less advertisements in a Spex issue than in any DJ magazine. The reviews of the latest releases in popular music culture are sorted alphabetically. There are also some side issues like "serious rap affairs" which specializes on the latest rap releases or "wasteland" which deals with music from frank black to hovercraft. Another astonishing fact

---

[7] vgl. Dufresne, David: Yo! Rap Revolution. Geschichte. Gruppen. Bewegung. Edition Ramsay. Mai 1992. S. 158ff
[8] Jacobson, Harlan: Wild Style, in: film comment. Juni 1983. S.66
[9] Dath, Dietmar: ägypten ist nicht Egypten. In: Spex. Nr. 04/99. Köln 1999. S.40

is that the magazine does not simply reduce its character to music issues – you can also find articles about Sadie Plant and a critique of cyber feminism and female understanding of technology or stories about pop theatre. The content cannot be reduced to mixing skills, since it is a connecting thread to an intellectual thinking youth culture.

In Austria a similar magazine is published. It is called SKUG and its undertitel is "subversive moments in music". It is written in a similar style than the Spex, but the layout is a little bit more minimal. The Skug magazine also deals with topics like films, musical television, latest book releases, artfiles – a discourse about art and the public – and contains about 40 pages full of music reviews. The interviews and reports basically deal with Austrian bands or producers, but also international stars like the WU-TANG CLAN or MOUSE ON MARS are included.

These two magazines should only be examples for the existence of intellectual music magazines in Europe which refer to a specific understanding of sub- and youth culture. They differ from strict DJ magazines, because of the wider range of topics and they also refer to another target group. They often pick up trends and reflect them on a higher level of understanding. For instance, the development of German hip hop music was discussed and got established through its presentation within these magazines.

The music journalists who are writing for these magazines as well as for DJ magazines have occupied themselves a lot with the topics they are writing about and know about what they are talking.

VII.) Conclusion – DJ Culture as postmodern or height-modern movement

Finally, it has to be said that DJ culture cannot be summarized in just one sentence. I has developed itself throughout the last centuries with different directions. Hip Hop, Breakbeat and Drum'n'Bass are just parts of this development which used the typical instruments of DJ action: two turntables and an MC (Master of Ceremony) to cut, unite and mix sounds, to scratch and to present content within the vocals.

"Whatever the respective musical and political merits of these new departures, or the scale of their influence, they can be argued to be postmodern. They are concerned with collage, pastiche and quotation, with the mixing of styles which remain musically and historically distinct, with the random and selective pasting together of different musics and styles, with the rejection of divisions between serious and fun or pop music and with the attack on the notion of rock as a serious artistic music ....”[10]

Dominic Strinati, a lecturer in Sociology at the University of Leicester in the United Kingdom, defines DJ culture as postmodern, because different styles of music are mixed. In contrast to postmodern music Strinati regards modern music as an attempt to fashion new and distinct styles out of previous forms.

In contrast, the author of the often quoted book "DJ culture" is not sure if postmodernism really is the goal of unlimited opportunities.

"In postmodern culture, "culture" has become a product in its own right; the market has become a substitute for itself and fully as much a commodity as any of its items it includes within itself: modernism was still minimally and tendentially the critique of the commodity and the effort to make it transcendent itself. Postmodernism is the consumption of sheer commodification as a process."[11]

This statement by Frederic Jameson takes Adorno's thesis about culture industry as root position for further thoughts and does regard the commercialization of musical underground trends as fact which cannot be denied.

In opposition to that, Ulf Porschardt creates in his book "dj culture" a new expression, called height-modernism and is meant as a mixture of the positive aspects of modernism and postmodernism. DJ culture does adopt old musical styles which is regarded as modernistic and creates something new with its mixing, which is regarded as postmodern. Therefore DJ cannot be defined as modern or post-modern at all and Mr. Porschardt developed a new term. For instance, hip hop culture can be regarded as the next big step after the black panther movement into a proud, intellectual self-determination of the Afro-American population in the United States. "Knowledge is king" is the statement of a rap song by Kool Moe Dee which shows clearly how necessary it is to learn more about the world and how many questions are still open and not answered within society. [12]

---

[10] Strinati, Dominic: popular culture. An introduction to theories of popular culture. Routledge. London 1995. S.234
[11] Jameson, Frederic: Postmodemism. S. ix. in: Porschardt, Ulf: ebda. S. 404

We still live in revolutionary times, because hip hop music and culture has not changed the social situation in the ghettos yet. During the last two centuries the situation of minorities in the United States has not changed immensely. The number of black children who grew up in poverty arose from 41, 2 per cent to 43,7 per cent and the life expectancy of black men who live in ghettos is still lower than those of men who live in so-called "third world" countries.[13] Hip Hop DJs and MCs still use these themes in their raps and the lyrics are full of social critique. As long as these people make aware of such problems, there is still a little hope for change.

Literature List:

Arnell, Richard: Krust. in: knowledge 2/12. November 1999. Vision Publishing. Bristol 1999

Dath, Dietmar: Ägypten ist nicht Egypten. In: Spex. Nr. 04/99. Köln 1999

Dufresne, David: Yo! Rap Revolution. Geschichte. Gruppen. Bewegung. Edition Ramsay. Mai 1992

Hughes, Walter: Feeling Mighty Real. In: Rock'n'Roll Quarterly. Sommer 1993

Jacobson, Harlan: Wild Style. in: film comment. Juni 1983

Poschardt, Ulf: DJ Culture – Diskjokeys und Popkultur. Rowohlt. Reinbek bei Hamburg. Oktober 1997

Strinati, Dominic: Popular Culture. An introduction to theories of popular culture. Routledge. London 1995

---

[12] Vgl. Porschardt, Ulf: ebda. S. 406ff
[13] Vgl. Porschardt, Ulf: ebda. S. 417f